Diaries of the mentally ill and slightly deranged

TURNING PAIN INTO PROSPERITY

Marilyn Night

Ashley J Andrews

Marilyn Night

To each and every soul that has ever felt like their life doesn't matter.
You are not alone, you do matter and fuck whoever made you feel
otherwise!

Contents

1

The little girl

2

No voice

3

Praying for light

4

Night madness with the monsters

Contents - v

Live for yourself

24
Worth the fight

25
Love

26
He who accomplished the impossible

27
Loving me isn't easy

28
Tomorrow is never promised

29
Because I love you

30
Will you sign on the dotted line?

31
The warrior and the knight

A little about me

Ok so. I figured I would explain how this book of crazy ass poetry came about. I put them in order the best way I could, but when it comes to me and my life there is not much order. Well, unless it is from a menu ha-ha. Anyways, I would like to say that I did not have the worst life imaginable. There are a million others who have had it far worse than I did, but it damn sure was not a skip through a meadow on a spring day either.

I have been through enough to know that there is truth in the saying, "What doesn't kill you makes you stronger." It does not feel that way when you are in the eye of the storm, but when the rain clears, the dust settles, and you are still standing then that is a win in my book. Even if it is with one shoe on, some dirty ass jeans and a fucked-up hairdo. That only means you stood against that storm instead of allowing it to break you.

I have been fighting storms for as long as I can remember. As a result, I developed an array of disorders, and two just so happen to have names of their own ha-ha. I have hidden in closets while my mother took an ass whooping. I ran away in the middle of the night in just a nightgown and no shoes on, to get away from a babysitter who had been doing things to me that not any five-year old should have to experience. It was not until many years later when I decided that I should get some help that I became aware of the damage that was caused by these events.

VICTORIA

I was about five years old when my little Victoria came to be. Whenever there was something happening that I did not need to be present for I would kind of just "go away" I would play with Vic then when it was safe to return, my time with Vic is all I would remember.

The trauma had caused my brain to create a way for me to escape scary situations. I thought she was a normal imaginary friend and would go away as I got older. Not my little Vic, she is still with me.

She stayed a little girl even though I grew up. She tends to make her way out when I am in an exceptionally good mood. When I come back to myself, I usually have a new painting and messes to clean up Ha-ha.

It has not always been all fun and games when she has come out though. For most of my adult life I have been embarrassed of her. She would come out at the most inconvenient times. She experiences what I do. So, if adult things are happening, and I have not blocked her from it, I end up in the fetal position, crying uncontrollably, having flashbacks accompanied by a panic attack.

So yea embarrassed does not even cover it. I had wished so many times that she would just go away so that I could just be "normal." Now I would be devastated if that were to happen. I love her like I would any other best friend that I have had for the better part of thirty years. She is a part of me and without her I would not be whole.

NICOLE

Though I grew up in a war zone, I do not like conflict. I am a lover not a fighter, but when you grow up with a stepdad like I had that does not matter in the least. You are going to fight like it or not, and cry, O hell no, you better not. That just makes you a pussy that needs to toughen up.

I was about eleven or twelve when I did just that. He was screaming, I was crying and yelled "I hate you" to him. Next thing you know I am being pinned to the door with his hand around my throat. He called me a little fucking cunt and that is the last thing I remember.

When I came back to myself it was all over. I had a headache, and he had a bloody face and sore balls. From that night forward any time I got to a certain level of anger I would black out and when "I" came back whoever had pushed me to that point was not in the best shape. I guess that night my little brain said screw this shit and created a fighter to defend me.

I call her the warrior, but her name is Nicole. She did not reveal the fact that she had a name of her own Until I was in my twenties though. Up until then I just thought she was "the devil on my shoulder." The voice in my head that always wanted to fuck shit up ha-ha. I thought I was coo coo for coco puffs, because I would have full-fledged arguments with her in my head trying to keep her from taking control.

It is fascinating how the brain works. It is even more confusing. When I try to think back on my life there is a lot that is foggy. Then there are parts that I cannot remember at all. Gaps in time where it seems like I was not even there.

Which I was not if you think about it, but that is a rabbit hole I try not to get lost in. One thought leads to another and next thing you know I am questioning my entire existence. Going through pictures like a "crazy person" trying to piece it together.

STORMS

This life has taken me through many ups and downs, and I have learned MANY lessons. It calloused me and made me cold and untrusting. During the good times I would question every aspect, wondering when the storm was going to hit. If I was happy and not just content in my day-to-day misery, I mean truly happy. That's when I knew a shit storm was about to come swirling in like a hurricane, leaving me devastated, piecing my life back together. It was not a matter of IF; it was a matter of WHEN.

I've struggled with depression, self-harm and attempted suicide more times than I can count. I decided to see a professional in 2017 and was diagnosed with borderline personality disorder, bipolar, insomnia, ptsd, dissociative identity disorder, severe depression, and severe anxiety. I took, if I remember correctly, nine different medications three times a day. Sadly, the only one that helped is the anxiety medication. All my problems remained, and I was put on mental disability in 2018.

During this time, I started seeing my now ex-husband. I fell for him instantly and hard. Every brick from that meticulously built wall came crashing down around me. The first year and a half was full of ups and downs, around the end of 2018 we moved from our hometown to a small town where his family lives to get a fresh start. He was sober and everything was going great. So great that we decided to get married in March of 2019.

I was happier than I had ever been. So happy in fact that I didn't see the shit storm that was about to hit coming.

Around six months or so after the wedding the clouds started rolling in. I saw the" ready to run" look in his eyes, He was on the verge of relapse. I made a decision that night that would change my life forever.

I was not ready to let go of our newfound happiness, so I made him a deal. If it would keep him from starting fights so that he could get away to do what he wanted. If it would keep him from putting me through the same bull shit as before, then I would do it with him. Even though doing so would mean throwing away over ten years of sobriety from drugs.

I hoped that he would say no. I trusted that he loved me enough that he would not let me do that. Sadly, I overestimated his love and underestimated the power drugs had over him. So those years of sobriety went right down the crapper. A few weeks later here came the shit storm, but not the normal kind of shit storm I was used to. No No this was the F5; the one that brought complete devastation and death!

Everything that I had ever done in my past relationships was handed right back to me ten times over. I was in hell! Manipulation was the game, and I was the target. Being gas lighted and made to believe that I was going crazy (well crazier anyway).

I hated myself for being so weak. For knowing what was being done but staying anyway. More than anything I hated myself for loving another person more than I loved myself. More than I loved my own fucking life. I couldn't even look in the mirror. I was disgusted with what looked back at me; I said "what" because it was an empty lifeless corpse, it was not me!

This went on for about a year or so. Getting worse by the day. Then on New Year's Eve of 2020 during yet another argument, one where I voiced a concern and him informing me that I was wrong. I told him that I couldn't handle much more. That I was to the point that I just didn't feel like living any longer. I made the statement that I should just kill myself.

He then reached on top of our Refrigerator and took a brand-new razor blade out of the box. He looked me dead in the eyes as he handed it to me, and said, "then fucking do it already". I never broke eye contact as I took the razor from him, extended my left arm and in one single motion sliced from wrist to mid arm.

I looked down at my arm and seen that the cut was deep enough that at first there was almost no blood, just tiny specks of it throughout the white flesh. Then within seconds it started gushing out. I realized in that moment that I may in fact bleed to death.

I calmly stood up, walked to the bathroom and swallowed two half-filled bottles of the medications that were supposed to help prevent this type of thing. Then I laid down on the floor and waited to die.

A few seconds later the door opened. He looked down at me and said, "you aren't dead yet"? He then closed the door and walked away. I could barely take a breath at this point, and I could only feel my heartbeat one beat at a time. Then everything went dark!

As the darkness consumed me, I felt all those terrible emotions that others had felt because of me. It felt as if I were being crushed by the weight of it all. Somehow in that moment I knew that everything that I had gone through was my karma.

You think going through shit like this sucks? Well, I will let you in on a little secret. Finding out that you deserved every bit of it really bites the big one! It is a fucking eye opener for damn sure!

While all of this is happening a voice that I had never heard before screamed through the darkness. A scream so loud that it could have shattered windows. The voice was telling me that I was selfish, that my children deserved to have their mother. I had never been much of a believer in God or angels. Hell, I never had faith in anything but myself actually, but I was pretty sure that the voice was an angel and boy was he pissed.

I started praying to that voice and anyone that could hear me and was listening. I prayed for my life, I made the promise that if I was given another chance, I would live my life differently and I would never attempt to cut it short again.

I woke up on my couch almost four days later, my arm had been taped shut and bandaged and I was ALIVE. I don't know how I got there or what exactly happened after I prayed, but I do know one thing for sure. I was given a second chance and for that I thank God and that angel every day.

Since that day I have lived my life differently just as I promised. I wrote letters of apology to anyone I could remember doing wrong and forgiveness letters to those who had wronged me. I do not intentionally hurt anyone, and I apologize if I do by accident. I wake up every day knowing that my life has value and purpose, and God and his Angels have my back even on the bad days.

I never want to feel what I felt that night in the darkness again! I'm pretty sure where I was headed had I not asked for forgiveness was not the place that I want to end up. The only way to ensure that that does not happen is to be kind to others, and to live honestly. To love myself enough to know that it is ok to distance myself from those who cause me pain or sadness. Above all else have faith in God, his angels and in myself.

Now I'm not saying that you have to go to church and be a prude. Personally, I do not agree with organized religion. What I mean is if you live honestly and with only good intentions, if you show kindness and compassion even to those who do not show it to you and make sure god knows that your faith is in him. Things will start to slowly get better and Karma will take care of those who choose to treat you poorly when the time is right. Whatever you put out, you will receive in return good or bad. So, in other words live the way you want your life to be.

I'm not saying that it has been all sunshine and rainbows either. The following year got pretty shitty, but I kept my faith, prayed every day for it to get better and done the things I needed to do to help that process. That was three years ago, and I can honestly say that if you can show God that you have trust in him even through the hard times, he will bless you with all the peace and happiness you deserve.

Crazy Town

These emotions are exhausting!
Franticly changing more and more
often.
Rapidly racing from the highest
point of happy
Then descending to the deepest
depths of despair.
Rounding the corner to crazy town,
I spend most of my time there.
Others don't quite understand me.
Most don't even try.
Choosing only to focus on the
differences between us.
Never caring enough to ask or
listen to the how or why.
People fear what they do not
understand.
Walking away is easier than forcing
their minds to expand.

1

The little girl

Who would have ever guessed that she would grow up to be such a mess?

The sweet little girl with those big brown eyes. The one that hides in the closet and silently cries.

She doesn't like it when they fight!

When things get physical and momma cries.

Momma put some clothes in a bag. "Please don't make me go" she thinks. Daddy looks sad sitting in his big chair, holding her favorite teddy bear.

He gives her a hug and tells her she can stay. "If you don't want to go, I won't let momma take you away!"

She is so confused. What should she do?

She loves her momma and her daddy too.

She doesn't understand why she must choose.

She is made of demon
whispers and angel tears,
razorblade scars and
childhood fears.

The only thing as dark as her
coal-colored eyes is her tainted
decaying heart.

I fear no monster, it is impossible you
see; The scariest monster I know is a
part of me. She is my closest friend and
my single worst enemy

2

No voice

She speaks with passion about music, poetry, books, and art. She stops short and gives an apology for speaking at all.

Hurtful people throughout her life broke her spirit and snuffed out her light.

Ignoring her words always last, never put first. Making her feel like she wasn't worth their time.

Conditioned to keep quiet and never speak her mind.

They couldn't put out the light in her soul, they only dulled the shine.

Pen and paper became her best friends.

The words are forever there along with the passion that fuels them.

She doesn't mind because now they can never be lost or forgotten.

Her thoughts, her dreams and all of the in-betweens will be right there on paper for someone to one day read.

3

❧

Praying for light

Life is but a fleeting glimpse, consumed by the night.
Staring at the moon, praying for light.
Light to shine down and take away the fright.
The fright of the fight for life.
The fright of the unknown, grief and strife.
Shed light; show me the light.
Please don't let the darkness swallow me alive.

4

Night madness with the monsters

Silence all around me, only the music in the background delaying the insanity .

Meaningless conversation stuck on replay day after day. Never going too deep, staying always on the surface.

They think they are playing me, but like a Polaroid I'm always in focus.

Feelings are not welcome here; emotions are the enemy. Fear, regret, sadness and anger are all I see.

Empty corpses, bones and skin.

There is no depth to them.

Hollow eyes, no light within.

Tricksters playing head games. Assuming that I don't see plain.

Mistakenly forgetting that I to have monsters waiting to be put in the game.

I just keep them locked away.

Their hunger grows more every day. Waiting patiently for their chance to play.

I can hear their snarls, breath growing heavier, baring their teeth.

Excitement building, it's almost their time to eat.

Their thoughts flash visions in my head.

Blood, Fire, Destruction! Then all Red!

"Soon my loves" I assure them that their time grows near.

I must be strategic and precise, while I walk this fine line.

Losing the good within myself while playing in hell is my only fear.

One Part angel, the other part demon.

Appearing the same but we are so very different!

The angel wants nothing but peace and love, but the demon is 100% ruthless and out for blood!

If her coal black eyes appear, it's probably best you run! The demon is the angel's pet.

Push the angel over the edge and the demon is who you'll get!!

I have nothing to hide and nothing I feel the need to reveal. A listening ear with enough ammo breeds an enemy. So, I keep my cards close, and my mouth closed! Just in case the snake comes disguised as a friend to me

May they all choke on the smoke from the fire in my soul. All who's words ever took a toll. May they see the scars and know in their hearts that words paired with actions can rip someone apart.

5

The player

Do you enjoy seeing me suffer?

To you, it's all a game. I'll cut a little deeper, then tomorrow be ashamed!

Wipe that stupid grin off your face!

Could you handle even half? Or would you buckle under the weight?

Do you love me enough to take it all away? To save my life would you stand in my place?

It's not a singular moment, nor one particular person that is the cause for all this pain.

There is simply life to blame!

The first cut brings a sigh of relief.

The blood flows as the suffering held inside gets released.

The physical pain helps to drown out the emotional strain.

We three share this burden.

Though in times like these, it is only I who hold the reins!

I am not Marilyn, she is not to blame, and I am not Victoria, of me she is ashamed.

We are not the same!

I am Nicole, and it is I who will determine our fate.

6

Losing myself

I have fought my demons to the brim,

but it is not a battle I think I can win!

This thing that beats inside my chest;

has lost the fight but tried its best.

There is no point in my existence!

I can't control my life. I am merely a witness.

I've lost myself again!

I'm not sure if I will be back this time; maybe it's the end!

Body, soul, heart and brain; grow weaker by the day.

Each time I lose myself, the longer I stay.

It seems inevitable; that sometime soon,

my mind will drift away, never to return.

No one will care! I've never mattered much anyway!

Not one person has ever fought for me to stay.

Not a single soul that has hurt at the thought of me going away.

Like a puppy that no one wants. I am just a stray!

Head packed full of memories
As vast and deadly as the ocean
Never silent, never giving relief

Memories engulf me
Emotions take over
Pain sets me free

I can handle the pain
The voices drive me insane
Steeling my nights
Haunting my days

7

My own prisoner

In the dead of night and wee morning hours

questions consume my head

for answers it scowers.

Sleep never comes easily, now the day lumes over me.

Towering like a giant preparing to crush me.

It's a tremendous fist forged from worry and doubt.

Will it always be this hard?

Will I ever make it out?

My heart longs for a day of relief.

Will it ever come?

Will I ever find peace?

From my own minds chains will I ever be released?

Or bound for life shall I forever be?

Imprisoned by my demons until deceased.

8

Warrior

I get quiet, sometimes.

heavy is the weight that is bound to my heart.

Once in a while it gets grizzly inside.

war-torn, tattered, beat down and battered.

Thoughts get messy emotions grow testy.

Time with myself is often what is best for me.

To gather all the scattered pieces

Then tuck them away for safekeeping.

Tend the wounds and regroup.

So, I can quickly get back to being me.

So just kick back and don't worry.

when my voice goes silent, and my eyes fill with Fury.

Growing ever so darker until they are as black as coal.

It is then that I am engulfed in the flames.

Dwelling deep within my soul.

A fire forged by all those who ever doubted me.

Those who threw away my love

Those who turned their backs on me.

They were Giving me all the strength I would ever need!

I am a warrior, tried and true.

Life is war. that's nothing new.

I will not be defeated; I wear these scars proudly to prove.

I was built for battle through and through!

9

Stitch me back together

Cuts, stitches, staples: Don't feed me any fables!

No tall tales to try and turn the tables.

She doesn't believe in fairy tales.

No knight in shining armor.

She is the monster!

She dwells with the demons that he has come to slay.

She is the dragon!

Ready to incinerate those brave enough to get in her way!

Words of wisdom to those who dare to try.

To face the inferno that within her heart lies.

If you only live and love for the day

just step aside and stay out of her way!

Honor, integrity, honesty, respect!

She knows what she deserves and will settle for nothing less!

The fire within her soul can only be tamed.

by the one who's heart harbors these qualities without shame.

The one that can stitch together those broken pieces.

others left in their wake.

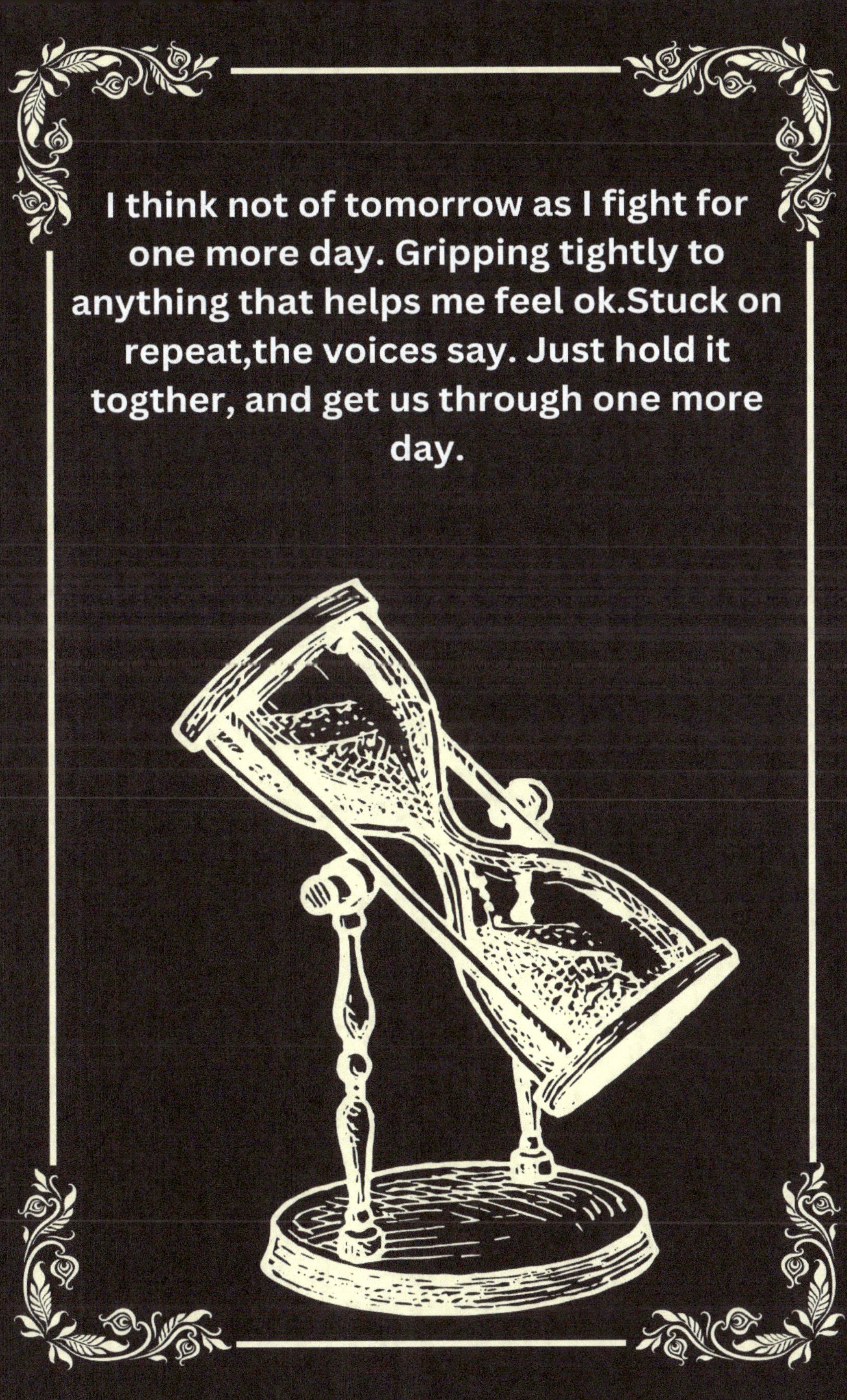

I think not of tomorrow as I fight for one more day. Gripping tightly to anything that helps me feel ok.Stuck on repeat,the voices say. Just hold it togther, and get us through one more day.

10

Never enough

What is wrong with me?

Why am I never enough?

Knowing this

Why do I still let myself trust?

Knowing that it is never more than lust.

Being used for a little while

Then left in the dust.

Leaving me depressed

Once again asking the question

Will I ever find love?

11

Who will it be?

A handful of pills to start the day.

Doctors attempt to keep the demons away.

Just for a short while, of course.

alarm sounds.

It's time for more.

"She is insane", they claim.

Take these meds three times a day!

They will keep your demons at bay.

"They don't work," I say!

They still want to come out and play.

Ominous dreams and sinister thoughts.

How will this end?

What will be the cost?

There are three of us who fight to be "boss".

The ultimate price for each is not the same.

Though we all three end up in the same place.

With which one of us will life take its toll?

Locked inside one head, but all sharing the same soul.

So, when we meet the ferryman, our beloved Mr. Reaper.

Who will be the puppet master as the others are safely sleeping?

Will our dear friend be paid with Marilyn's unwavering love?

Will Victoria pay with her fear and distrust?

Or will it be Nicole that pays the reaper's toll?

With anger and resentment, proudly worn as armor.

ready to go to battle in an instant.

I suppose it shall remain a mystery; until that day arrives.

When we three climb aboard the ferry

Starting our journey to the other side.

12

Behind my eyes

It's crazy the way life takes a turn.

One day you're a young girl trying to find your way.

Then in the blink of an eye you're all grown up.

praying that you make it through one more day.

How fast time flies but still sometimes

I catch a glimpse if I look just right.

That little girl is still there.

behind my eyes she hides.

Bound to me forever

in my mind she resides.

Sitting at a table with an older angrier version of herself.

Radio to the right, coloring book to the left.

Neither visible to the naked eye

 You will catch a glimpse sometimes

if you look into my eyes just right.

The two I have grown to love.

My companions for life.

War

Born in a time of war, she was raised doing battle. Indomitable, she stood fearless in the face of an enemy. Her nerve could not be rattled! Comfortable standing on the front line, she knew ground zero all too well. A sweet little girl evolved into a savage warrior from a life lived too long in hell.

13

Disgrace

I look in the mirror and I am disgusted with what I see.

That is not ME.

The empty shell of what was once a beautiful queen.

Now so meek, so tiny, so weak!

You are disgusting, A FUCKING DISGRACE!

I say as I spit in her face.

How dare you let this sad, tired bitch take the queen's place!

You wonder why you feel no love.

Look at what you have become!

You don't even love yourself.

Why the fuck would anyone else!

14

When the monster whispers

Darkness calls

The monster whispers.

In the moonlight, the sharp blade glistens

Engulfed in emotion, it is now that I call to the

Help me, Nicole

Take this pain from me.

I beg of you!

Please, please!

I relinquish control.

Come set me free!

our greatest fear is our only relief.

Until painfully we wake

Once again in disbelief.

15

Find a release

My thoughts are constantly reeling.

I am filled with emotion plumb to the ceiling.

I Sort them out and write them down.

From my heart and mind, they are unbound.

This helps to ease the painful feelings.

Only then can I begin healing.

Poems, quotes, and crazy little notes.

Bringing light into the dark.

Replacing it with hope.

Then I add that page to the story being told.

Terrified to love, she pushes away anyone
that tries to get close. Fearful of the pain th
can cause, so scared of the possibility of los
She would rather hurt herself than let
someone else break her heart.

*Dusk came quietly, as the dark of night
followed. She knew she belonged to him! No
one knows darkness as well as he and no-
one could silence its oblivion as well as she.*

Will you still want me when face to face wit
my rage or will fear grab hold of you as you
scramble from my cage? On the surface I
look timid and sweet but do not be deceive
What dwells in the depths beneath is
something you should pray you never get t

16

Tick-Tock

Come sit down, let's have a talk.

Tick-Tock Tick-Tock

I ask a question

A blank stare or a head nod I get in response

Tick-Tock Tick-Tock

I let a little time pass and give it another go

Zip-Zilch-Nada

Anger rushes from head to toe

I take a deep breath and let it out slow

Anger will fix nothing, go away Nicole

Tick-Tock Tick-Tock

The bull shit never stops

My brain explodes

Pop-Pop

Mental issues that just don't stop

17

The last night

It was fate that brought them together, karma at its finest. Their eyes met and it was over. He had her by the heart. Five short years later, His eyes had turned cold and dark. The love he once felt for her was gone. His words ugly and painful. Like the razor in her hand, deadly and sharp. He would drive her to near madness. Then smirk and smile at her breaking heart. He enjoyed causing her pain. Manipulation was his favorite game. On that cold December night, she couldn't take anymore. What remained of her laid curled up in a tiny ball on the blood-stained floor. Her quiet sobs for help were paid no mind. He looked down at her once more. His heart cold as ice, he shut the door. He didn't realize as he walked away that where he left her is where she would stay. Only the memory of her would remain.

18

She is no more

You inject self-doubt into my veins.

Fucking up my mentality with all your little games

Leaving me questioning my own sanity.

I have become my own worst enemy

Walking around aimlessly!

I am at war with my body every day.

I try to scrub your harsh words away

but in my mind and heart they stay.

I don't know who I am now.

Who I once was has faded away.

A woman once so brave and full of life.

Now broken and sad, lay dying in the floor.

She is no more!

you are
your reason!

you are worth it!

Fuck what they think!

You are beautif...

It can get better!

Love yourself!

...ever give up!

there is Al...
Hope

I wear your words on my body. Even when memory fades, they will still not be forgotten.

I await the night, run to the darkne... Beneath its veil I a... hidden from the heartless.

you cringe and turn away at the sight of my scars. Torn up legs and mangled arms. What you cannot see through judgmental eyes and a cold heart is that the love I have

19

No more tears

I begged and I fucking pleaded.

even got down on my knees.

So many times, I cried, and I screamed.

please just love me or just let me fucking leave!

like a coward you just turned your cheek.

You say that I have no reason to feel the way I do inside.

you have no empathy and way too much pride.

You lie and you cheat.

Then you deny and turn it around on me.

You put yourself on that pedestal.

All high and fucking mighty.

blinding yourself to the fact that losing me was likely.

You do not care about the words I express.

Sitting so high up on that horse.

With all that pride in your chest.

Does it get chilly?

just a tad bit lonely?

All alone with your thoughts.

All fake and phony.

I loved you so much!

I would have died before leaving.

As a Matter of fact, I did just that.

You didn't even try to save me!

I woke days later with great clarity.

The person I should love that much is me!

You only cared for yourself.

You never took me seriously.

You just sat there emotionless.

Convinced that I would stay.

Not caring at all that you were pushing me away.

Now you act so surprised.

Like my leaving came out of the blue.

Now that I'm gone.

 You're only lying to you.

To be Loved and shown respect.

To be given affection, not neglect.

That's all I ever wanted.

 You've shown me for the last time.

That to you I'm not worth it.

I will not ever shed another tear.

for a man that does not deserve them!

20

A love of my own

I just want to someone to love me, is that too much to ask?

Someone to love away all the wounds and scars from the past.

I wish for and hope to have one day.

A love that will last, a love that will stay.

A love of my very own.

One that i don't have to share with another.

One that does not feel like my love is a bother.

No manipulation, no gas lighting or any other form of abuse.

I've had my fair share of that so called love.

I'm calling a truce!!

Someone to drink coffee with while we watch the sun rise.

Someone that doesn't even have to say a word,

I can see it in their eyes.

21

Reborn

So many years spent feeling not good enough.

A lifetime wasted feeling not worthy of love.

So much worry, am I giving enough?

While all along I was giving too much!

Too much thought, and too much energy.

Taking years but eventually

Draining the life right out of me, slowly but efficiently.

Everyone else's thoughts and opinions plagued me.

The end of that Era I can only remember vaguely.

With the end of one life another came to be.

I thank God and his angels every day for saving me.

From myself and the mental hell that caged me.

Finally, I was set free!

Reborn; I woke with amazing clarity!

Somehow knowing that my life had meaning.

That it had purpose!

Knowing not a single soul should ever have to wonder.

Why those they give their love., deem them worthless and un-
worthy.

Aware that loyalty given is not always loyalty earned.

Those people will switch up and turn their backs on you.

Another lesson learned!

Though these things still hurt when the situations occur.

They no longer break me or make me question my own worth.

The actions and words of others are a reflection of themselves.

A glimpse into their own heart and simply nothing else!

I have never dealt with anything more complex or complicating than my own mentality . Trying to maintain daily sometimes gets the best of me.

Pain, heartache, fear and despair. Fury, madness and love not shared. Create a calloused heart and a cold blank stare.

I embrace the pain; it is the hand that reaches in and pulls me out of the darkness.

22

The only way over it is through it

Emotions show your weakness, making you vulnerable to your enemy That's what I was taught, so that's what I believed.

Now I know being emotional does not make me weak! You must be strong to feel everything so deeply!

Using drugs or alcohol to numb yourself.

Now that is the road that is easy, believe me!

Always keep your guard up and stay one step ahead you'll never lose a fight. That's what I was taught, so that's how I approached life.

Every relationship I entered prepared for battle. If I saw them flinch, I swung first.

There was nothing about me that could or would ever be seen as fragile.

I was a Warrior. My anger was my armor. Mean as hell and a whole lot stronger!

Then someone was sent to deliver my karma.

I fell hard!

All that heavy armor was stripped away with just one look.

I reached in, ripped it out, still beating, I handed him my heart.

Now I feel everything so deeply that sometimes it feels like my emotions are tearing me apart.

All the pain I had ever caused times ten i received.

Sadness, confusion and anger consumed me.

Then brought me to my knees. In that moment the confusion was gone, and the question of why was answered.

Everything happens for a reason, and the hard times we encounter hold a lesson.

23

Live for yourself

All these years spent feeling like an outcast.

The ones that I put before myself are the ones that put me last.

Talked down to and behind my back called names.

Their hateful words remain embedded in my brain.

Then by those same people being criticized for not being "sane".

The state of my mentality being used against me.

Did you know that B.P.D causes loss of hearing?

Did you know that being depressed and bipolar cause your vision to begin failing?

I should probably do some research, because that sure is news to me.

What do I know anyway?

I am just a crazy bitch that cannot hear or see!

Maybe they will gain recognition for their discovery.

Maybe they will name those side effects after me.

Then I can be mocked and shamed publicly.

To my face their true feelings are never admitted.

Only spouting their slander when they think I'm not listening.

But I catch them slipping.

They know nothing of honor or loyalty!

Treachery and treason are their way of life.

A loyal person's worst enemy!

A hard lesson learned, but not only will I be fine I will thrive!

Unlike them I've got me and mine!

I am walking away with no tears in my eyes, without anger or resentment, only a wave goodbye with my head held high.

I never imagined that home would end up somewhere I don't belong, but I have lived to please others for far too long!

I am nothing but grateful, because this life has made me capable and strong.

I will live it for only myself from this day on, like I should have been doing all along!

24

Worth the fight

This pain in my head is crippling. More each day my sanity keeps slipping.

Further into the abyss, now parts of me are missing.

I scream so loud, but no one is listening,

so I write it all down with quickness, with haste.

Before it all drifts away and with a voiceless void it is replaced.

If I can help just one, then this life was not a waste.

I once enjoyed it here; I wish I could have stayed.

But by my own thoughts and emotions I was betrayed.

Now in these pages portions of my soul are contained, and through my words I hope a memory of me remains.

I pray they reach out and touch lost souls like mine.

Life can be downright brutal dear ones, but I promise it's worth the fight!

Dedicated to the
woman that was there
for me when she
didn't have to be. My
bonus mom Hellyes
(Shellye). One of the
strongest women I
have ever known. She
was the meanest,
craziest, bitch you
could ever meet but
with the biggest heart.
FUCK CANCER!!!

When she self-destructs and wreaks havoc on herself, she is trying to destroy that thing inside of her that tears her apart.

My emptions run eternally deep. Even when I feel nothing, I feel it completely.

There is no fear in my heart, I cower before NO man! Firm and fearless is how I stand! I will only die quietly if by my own hand!

NEWER, HAPPIER, AND LESS FUCKED UP POETRY!

25

∾

Love

I wanted to know him.

To let him know me.

I could see the pain behind his smile.

I could feel the need for something solid in his touch.

I wanted to be that foundation.

That someone he could turn to in times of need.

I wanted to show him something I myself have never seen.

Loyalty that's endless.

Friendship that stands the test of time.

Most important LOVE!

THE PAINLESS KIND.

26

He who accomplished the impossible

There had never been anyone that could calm Nicole.

She is always ready for a fight.

Sarcastic and cynical but never quiet!

Until that night; you done the impossible.

I will never forget. You spoke and she grew silent.

Listening to every word.

No longer having the urge to rip out your throat.

She wanted to protect you.

She didn't want you to hurt.

This has never happened!

She hates everyone!

Vic and I were a little confused.

BUT

There is one thing that we know to be true.

She is meaner than both of us and she wants you.

Now you're stuck, I'm sure you see.

You lit the fire, hopefully you can handle the heat.

You don't just get one you poor bastard!

With us you get three!

27

Loving me isn't easy

I am not your " girl next door".

Not in any way your everyday " norm".

Inside my head is a vortex.

Backwards, all mixed up, and way too complex.

It's like going down that rabbit hole with Alice.

I've got more triggers than the Kardashians have asses.

If my mood is not to your liking, give it a few minutes.

The next one will be arriving.

I know to you this is all very confusing.

Maybe sometimes even a little amusing.

I will not expect that you fully understand why.

The likely hood of that happening is as highly unlikely as

that sly little rabbit learning to fly.

I will however ask you to please do your best to see.

That even though I'm an emotional, mixed up, basket case.

That is what makes me, Me!

I cannot change that, but i strive to be a little better each day.

So, if you are serious when you say you want to stay.

A loving heart, an open mind, and as much patience as you can possibly find. Will be what you need, if sticking around is what you decide.

There is no cure my love.

Me is who I will forever remain.

With all my heart and soul, I want you to know

Even when I am in an unsavory mood.

The love that I hold in my heart for you is true!

A love that neither time nor distance can fade or change.

I will love you without a single doubt until my dying day.

28

Tomorrow is never
promised

I have been a cheater, I have been cold hearted, and I've used others to get what I wanted.

But yesterday is gone, and tomorrow is never promised.

A drug dealer, a drug addict, a horrible friend, and a bad daughter.

But yesterday is gone, and tomorrow is never promised.

I have thrown love away, and treated people like they meant nothing.

But yesterday is gone, and tomorrow is never promised.

That girl is gone now, replaced by a woman.

That life left behind, I am forever looking forward!

I fell in love with you when you spoke, because I no longer felt alone.

Now in your arms is where I feel at home.

I have not a single doubt that next to you is where I belong.

We have both lived lives that left us calloused and guarded, but I have never felt a love this strong!

Our future is all I care about; the past cannot haunt us.

 So, to you I want to make a promise.

I will stand by your side and walk through this life with you with honor.

I will be strong for you, and together we can face this world head on.

Please believe me when I say this.

I will not leave you, and I cannot be taken.

You will never have to face another battle alone.

To you I vow my loyalty until our good lord calls us home!

29

Because I love you

As if dealing with my abundance of emotion was not tricky enough.

You came waltzing in and made me fall in love.

So now I feel all of yours along with mine.

So go right ahead and tell me that you're doing just fine.

Flash that little half grin that doesn't quite reach your eyes.

Sorry to break it to you baby, but your energy doesn't lie.

I can feel the shifts; it doesn't matter how hard you try to hide.

 It breaks my heart to see your beautiful smile subside.

To know something is bothering you but there isn't a damn thing that I can do.

It makes me wonder what good I am if I can't help to ease your pain.

I just want you to be happy and free of all those chains!

I would gladly take it all, so never again would you have to say that your smile was taken by another darkened day!

30

Will you sign on the
dotted line?

She is wild

She dances beautifully with chaos.

She glides effortlessly through insanity.

Are you brave enough to follow her into madness?

An eternity in her arms seems like only minutes.

Getting lost in her darkness is the only escape!

A place where there is no difference between night and day.

She cannot just take you, oh no; you must be willing to play!

Make your decision with the utmost care, turning back is not an option!

You will belong to her forever!

Oh Forever; such a very long time!

You need not worry, let any fear subside.

She means you no harm; it is endless pleasure she has in mind!

So, if you think that you can handle this little devil,

Just sign right here on the dotted line.

X_ _ _ _ _ _ _ _

31

The warrior and the knight

A girl and a boy born years apart.

yet somehow twins, two souls one heart.

We walk through life together even when miles apart.

Brother and sister, best friends from the start.

We may disagree, we may even fight,

but that only strengthens the bond between a warrior and a knight.

With an unbreakable bond, and an unwavering love.

When together in battle NOTHING can defeat us!

Dedicated to my Brother Bear, I love you.

To all the lost souls like mine

Email/website- marilynnight.pubsitepro.com

For anyone who needs someone to talk to who actually cares. Send me an email, and from there we can figure out a method of communication you are most comfortable with.

9 798218 067311